C000096286

THE

RAGE

JOURNAL

THE RAGE JOURNAL

Copyright © Summersdale Publishers Ltd, 2021

All rights reserved.

Text by Claire Berrisford

No part of this book may be reproduced by any means, nor transmitted, nor translated into a machine language, without the written permission of the publishers.

Condition of Sale
This book is sold subject to the condition that it shall not, by way of trade or otherwise, be lent, resold, hired out or otherwise circulated in any form of binding or cover other than that in which it is published and without a similar condition including this condition being imposed on the subsequent purchaser.

An Hachette UK Company
www.hachette.co.uk

Summersdale Publishers Ltd
Part of Octopus Publishing Group Limited
Carmelite House
50 Victoria Embankment
LONDON
EC4Y 0DZ
UK

www.summersdale.com

Printed and bound in China

ISBN: 978-1-78783-675-4

Substantial discounts on bulk quantities of Summersdale books are available to corporations, professional associations and other organizations. For details contact general enquiries: telephone: +44 (0) 1243 771107 or email: enquiries@summersdale.com.

THE

RAGE

JOURNAL

UN-SPIRATIONAL ACTIVITIES AND
QUOTES FOR THOSE WHO NEED TO VENT

summersdale

INTRODUCTION

Are you fed up with being told to take a deep breath to calm your nerves? Are you so completely *over* being advised to simply smile the stress away? Does forcing yourself to be mindful, grateful and full of sunshine make you want to scream?

If so, welcome to *The Rage Journal*. This book is your angry place. It understands that sometimes deep breathing just isn't going to cut it. Those petty frustrations of everyday life have a tendency to build up, and when they do – when your blood is boiling and you feel like you're one tiny inconvenience away from exploding – the only thing on this earth that's going to make you feel better is a good old-fashioned rant.

Use the prompts on the following pages to unleash your everyday rage in a healthy and 100 per cent satisfying way. By the time you finish this book, it should be battered, it should be a little bit broken, it might even be completely destroyed – but you'll feel so much better for it.

So, what are you waiting for? Grab your pen and get ready to rage!

ANGER IS

WONDERFUL.

IT KEEPS YOU GOING.

TERRY PRATCHETT

CHOOSE TO RAGE

This book is all about allowing yourself to feel the rage that you would normally try to supress – like when you have a terrible time on public transport and it ruins your day, or you're late because you were stuck behind some slow walkers and it makes you want to punch a wall.

These are classic examples of things that cause everyday rage – the tiny, annoying things that build up over time and eat away at your mood. You might feel silly for getting mad at these little things, because there are so many other, bigger problems in the world, right?

Right. It's true. There are *most definitely* bigger problems than the fact that somebody walking slowly made you late. But that doesn't change the fact that when these things happen, *in that exact moment*, you feel riled up and ready to scream. Just because your frustrations (probably) don't matter in the grand scheme of things, it doesn't mean you don't feel REALLY MAD.

So, just ignore the fact that your anger is petty. WHO CARES? Instead of simmering away and feeling cranky, take 10 minutes and **choose to rage**. Feel your feelings and then let them out so that you can be left in peace.

In the space below, write down the last thing you remember getting *really* mad about – the pettier the better. Describe the experience.

_____

_____

_____

_____

_____

_____

_____

Now, write down why your feelings were completely justified.

_____

_____

_____

_____

_____

_____

Today,
I choose
~~joy~~
REALITY

I WANDER
ABOUT HATING
EVERYTHING
I BEHOLD.

LORD BYRON

RAGE SCALE

Here's another warm-up. Take a look at the scenarios below and rate how irritating they are on a scale of one to five – one being "I'm pretty chill about this" and five being "This makes me want to drop-kick something into the sun".

RATING	1 😌	2 😐	3 🙁	4 😠	5 😡
When the self-checkout doesn't register your items					
People who don't replace the toilet paper when it's run out					
When the voice recognition doesn't recognize your voice					
People who block the way in a shop aisle or on the pavement					
When you google something once and it is advertised to you for the next month					
People rustling in the cinema					
Impossible-to-open packaging					

RATING

	1 😊	2 😐	3 😟	4 😣	5 😠
People who eat with their mouth open					
When something catches on your earbuds and they get ripped out of your ears					
People who talk loudly on trains					
When you shake the sauce bottle and too much comes out					
Online videos being interrupted by adverts					
When a freshly sharpened pencil tip snaps					
Terrible hold music when you make a call					
When you try to pour something and it dribbles down the side					
When people ask for a bite of your food					
Stepping on an upturned plug					
When the bag of snacks rips in the wrong place and the rip just gets bigger and bigger...					
When people mispronounce words					
Buffering...					

The best
things in
life are ~~free~~

USUALLY
SUPER
EXPENSIVE

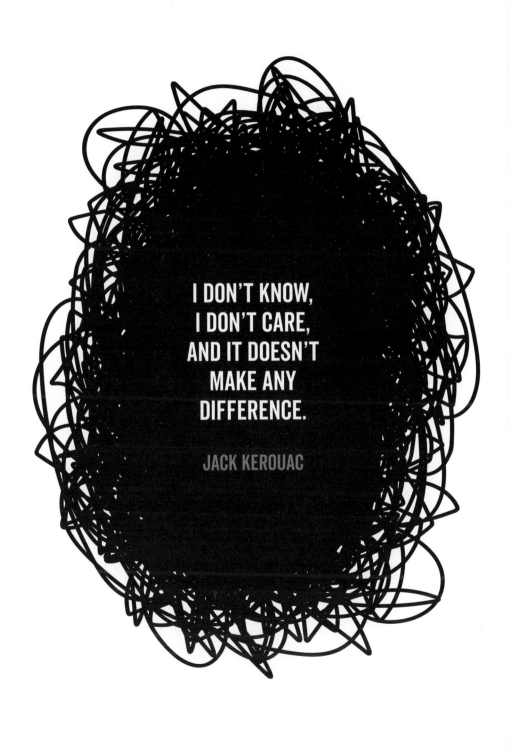

I DON'T KNOW,
I DON'T CARE,
AND IT DOESN'T
MAKE ANY
DIFFERENCE.

JACK KEROUAC

PET PEEVES

The last prompt should have got your creative juices flowing. Now use the space below to catalogue your own biggest pet peeves – the ones that get your blood well and truly lava-like. Sarcastic comments and sulky doodles are encouraged.

TEAM GLASS-HALF-EMPTY

I AM FREE OF ALL PREJUDICE.

I HATE

EVERYONE

EQUALLY.

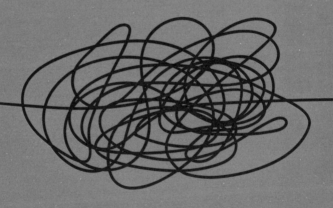

W. C. FIELDS

ANGER EXORCISM

Anger has a way of clinging on to you and munching away at your sanity, like some kind of hangry* demon. To find peace you've gotta cast that demon out and to do that – yep, you guessed it – you need to exorcize it with RAGE.

All you need to perform the exorcism is paper and a pen. Writing things down is powerful and cathartic, as it's a way to evict thoughts from your head and trap them on paper instead.

To begin your anger exorcism, pick a memory – a small injustice you keep coming back to, or something that was just so unbelievably dumb it makes you mad. Focus on that memory now and use the space below to describe it. Who was involved and what made it so infuriating? Give as much detail as you can. By the time you've finished, you should be able to breathe a sigh of relief.

* hungry + angry = hangry

WORD SEARCH

Unfortunately, the words you *really* want to shout when you're at your wit's end usually aren't appropriate for the situation. So here are some handy and completely innocent alternatives that are almost as satisfying. Find them in the word search opposite.

Pluck it

Frack

Sugar

Mother trucker

Shoot

Son of a bucket

What the duck

Fudge it

Holy sheet

Heck

S	T	T	I	U	A	H	E	J	H	D	W	B	C	K
P	O	N	I	V	N	K	E	O	B	Q	H	Z	N	C
M	D	N	E	E	C	M	L	C	F	A	A	U	E	A
H	T	C	O	Z	G	Y	V	L	K	D	T	S	F	R
R	K	Z	O	F	S	D	P	Z	R	O	T	E	Y	F
W	M	X	P	H	A	S	U	A	X	A	H	G	Q	N
G	M	J	E	E	Y	B	G	F	V	R	E	Q	O	E
A	Q	E	R	R	J	U	U	J	R	O	D	J	U	G
H	T	U	T	W	S	F	D	C	W	L	U	Z	L	X
L	S	H	O	O	T	W	Q	K	K	D	C	N	Q	L
B	W	H	S	Y	N	A	Y	L	U	E	K	B	I	R
Z	Z	N	Q	S	B	O	Y	U	J	I	T	U	Z	W
M	O	T	H	E	R	T	R	U	C	K	E	R	B	K
T	I	K	C	U	L	P	H	T	B	J	L	F	C	N
Q	C	J	W	G	J	I	Y	K	F	L	F	B	T	E

EXPRESS YOURSELF

It's not just words that have the power to cleanse us of our burning resentment – art has it too. Fortunately, you don't have to be da Vinci to benefit from this exercise.

First, take a moment to sit and think about a frustrating event. You could pick one of the pet peeves from a previous page and meditate on that, or you could choose something terrible that happened during your day. How did it make you feel? How much anger did you suppress? When you're good and ready and full of feelings, pick up your pen or paintbrush and unleash those feelings on to the page.

WHEN ALL IS SAID AND DONE, NOBODY CARES

Just look at this pattern.
It's so busy and bright white
and full of life – urgh. It's an
assault on your eyes and on your
raging soul. You need to make it
right. Colour this in in shades of
black and grey and impress your
angry feelings upon the page.

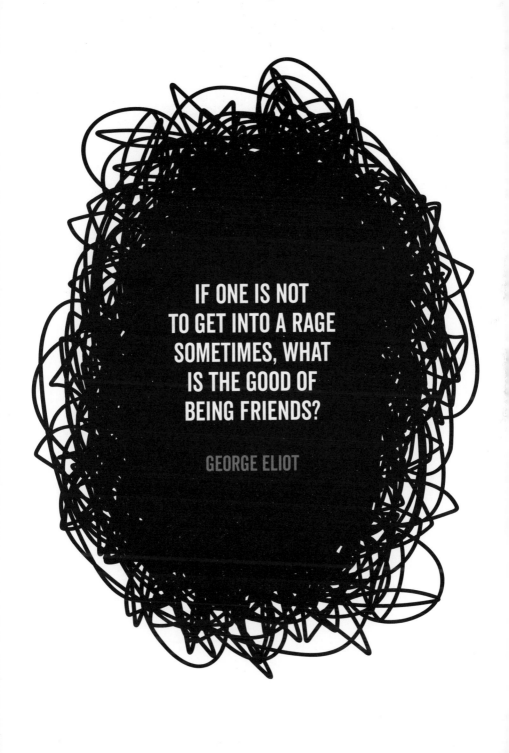

IF ONE IS NOT
TO GET INTO A RAGE
SOMETIMES, WHAT
IS THE GOOD OF
BEING FRIENDS?

GEORGE ELIOT

IDIOTIC TOP FIVE

This is a quick-fire round. Think of the top five most idiotic moments of the week. Did you leave a tissue in your pocket when you put your jeans in the wash? Did someone eat all the good chocolates from the box and leave the crap ones? Did your boss just come up with a "great idea" that you came up with three weeks ago? Three, two, one, GO!

1.

2.

3.

4.

5.

*INWARDLY
SCREAMING*

QUICK COMEBACKS

Rage gets you tongue-tied, and nothing – repeat – *nothing* is more humiliating than being in the middle of an argument and spluttering to a halt because your mind goes blank. But here you have a chance to reclaim your dignity.

Think back to your last enraging conversation and write all your most devastating comebacks below. (Who knows, you might even be able to use some of them next time.)

A GOOD PLACE TO PUT YOUR MOTIVATIONAL QUOTES IS... UP YOUR BUTT

DROP-KICK THIS BOOK ACROSS THE ROOM

WHAT HAS BEEN UNFAIR ABOUT TODAY?

Give yourself 5 minutes to think about all the things that have been awful and unfair about your day. This is your chance to moan and complain to your heart's content. Don't hold back now.

_____

_____

_____

_____

_____

_____

_____

_____

_____

_____

_____

Start and
end each
day with
~~positive vibes~~

A GOOD
RANT

BAD-MOOD BOARD

This is your mood board or, as this journal likes to call it, your bad-mood board. Use this space to draw all the things that make you SUPER MAD. You don't have to fill it up right away (unless you have a lot of things you want to get off your chest) – come back to it over time, add to it and expunge the rage from your soul.

Believe you can and you're ~~halfway there~~

PROBABLY KIDDING YOURSELF

TEAR OUT THIS PAGE AND THEN BURY IT IN THE GARDEN

IN THE WORDS OF HAMLET, ACT III, SCENE III, LINE 87, "NO"

ANONYMOUS NOTE

Everyone has at least one person who they wish they could walk up to and say what they *really* think. Unfortunately, being an adult means you have to "be polite" and "not make a scene" – but this is your rage journal and there's none of that here.

Think of the person who's really been getting on your nerves lately and use the space below to write them an anonymous note.

When it rains,
look for
~~rainbows~~

**AN
UMBRELLA**

LIFE DOESN'T GIVE YOU LEMONS – IT'S NOT GENEROUS ENOUGH

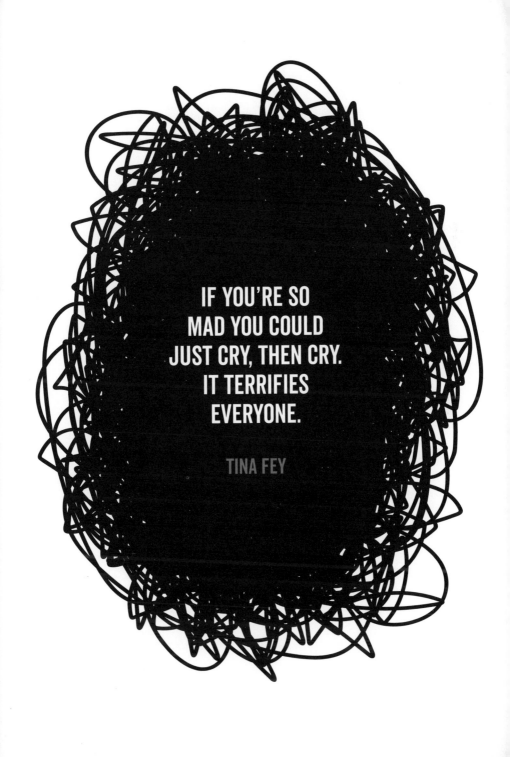

BLACKLIST PLAYLIST

Music has the power to make you feel a whole range of emotions... especially when it's a song that you hate. Write a list of all your least favourite, most despised songs – the ones that you never again want the misfortune of having in your earholes.

1. _____

2. _____

3. _____

4. _____

5. _____

6. _____

7. _____

8. _____

9. _____

10. _____

RIP OUT
THIS PAGE.
THEN RIP THE
PAGE INTO
TINY PIECES.

Go on. Rip it. *Do it.*

MAKE EVERY SECOND COUNT... OR COUNT EVERY SECOND UNTIL YOU CAN GET BACK INTO BED

SOME

~~Good~~

things are going to happen

I LOVE YOU, BUT...

You love your friends, right? Of course you do! But nobody's perfect. Even though they're better than most other people, your friends can still drive you absolutely crazy. Use this page to write down the most annoying things about your squad. If you feel the urge to get a little bit savage, that's okay. It's what this journal is here for. Just let it all out. (Although you might want to scribble over this with a marker when you're done...)

THE HALL OF SHAME

Disappointment is another face of rage. Think crisp packets being full of air. Chocolate chips that actually turn out to be raisins. Realizing you forgot to charge your phone overnight. URGH. This is a hall of shame for all the things that make you feel both disappointed and angry (a devastating combination).

EVERYTHING
IS STUPID

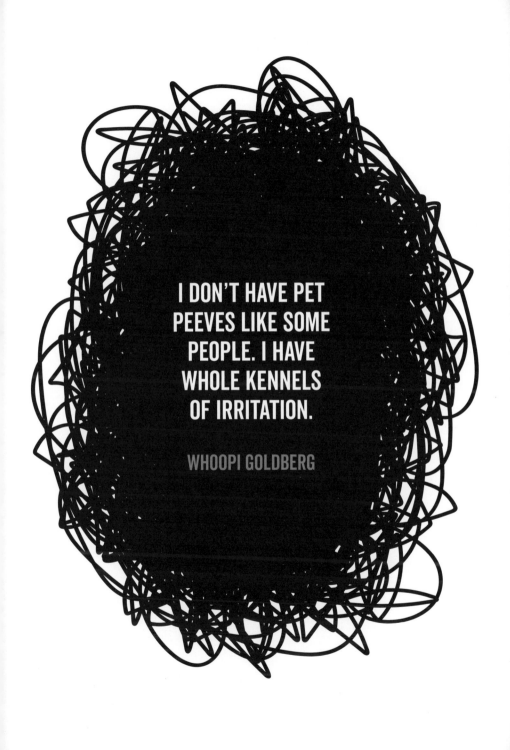

I DON'T HAVE PET
PEEVES LIKE SOME
PEOPLE. I HAVE
WHOLE KENNELS
OF IRRITATION.

WHOOPI GOLDBERG

THE ART OF THE EYE-ROLL

For those who favour passive-aggressive tactics to make themselves understood, eye-rolling is possibly the ultimate power move. A well-timed eye-roll is one of the most dramatic and badass non-verbal ways to signal things like, "This is stupid", "Stop talking, you're embarrassing yourself" or "I have nothing but pure contempt for this situation".

But it's not always the time and place for an eye-roll, if you want to, say, keep your job or stay on good terms with your family and friends. Try this instead: fill in each box opposite with a picture of someone or something that makes you want to eye-roll so hard you see your own brain. Then use the scale below to rate how big an eye-roll they deserve.

1	5	10
Subtle eye-roll of exasperation	Obvious eye-roll of supressed rage	Accidentally eye-rolled myself into another dimension

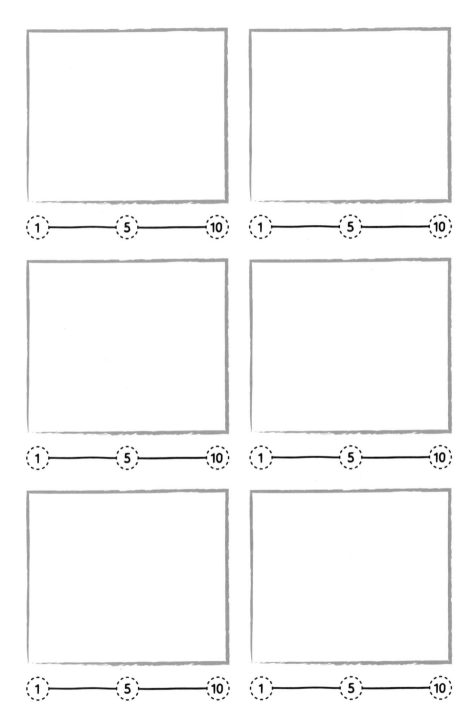

Smile and
the world will
~~smile with you~~

SEND BAD
KARMA
YOUR WAY

SCRIBBLE AND SCREAM ALL OVER THIS PAGE

TODAY'S FORECAST: MOODY WITH A 98% CHANCE OF SARCASM

RAGE REPLY

Nothing gets us raging like an irritating email. Maybe, yet again, you've been included in an unnecessary email with a CC list that's longer than *War and Peace*. Maybe you've received a message that's so astronomically frustrating you want to throw your phone across the room, then reply in full caps: NO, THIS EMAIL DOES NOT FIND ME WELL. ASDJGASJDHJAKJKLDJSD. Usually we don't have the sweet luxury of typing out what we really want to say, but here you have the freedom to vent. Think back to the last email that got you fuming and write out your ragiest, most chest-stabbingly blunt response.

To:

Subject:

SEND

A beautiful
day begins with
~~a beautiful~~
~~mindset~~
SILENCE

PICK A WORD — ANY WORD — THAT YOU LIKE TO SAY WHEN YOU'RE ANGRY. NOW WRITE IT IN BLACK MARKER OVER THE TEXT ON THIS PAGE IN REALLY HUGE LETTERS! (SAY/YELL THE WORD AS YOU WRITE FOR ADDED EFFECT.)

I LIKE LONG WALKS,
ESPECIALLY WHEN THEY
ARE TAKEN BY PEOPLE
WHO ANNOY ME.

FRED ALLEN

YOUR POSITIVITY MAKES ME WANT TO HIGH-FIVE YOU (IN THE FACE)

MAN THE LIFEBOATS.
THE IDIOTS
ARE WINNING.

CHARLIE BROOKER

IT'S A BEAUTIFUL DAY TO IGNORE OTHER PEOPLE

VERY ROTTEN TOMATOES

Use this page to write a list of all the films and TV programmes that you cannot stand. (Note: this can be especially satisfying if you passive-aggressively write in the journal whenever someone earnestly recommends that you "have to" watch a certain film or programme.)

I'D RATHER
BE SLEEPING
RIGHT NOW

I GET

ANGRY

ABOUT THINGS,
THEN GO ON
AND WORK.

TONI MORRISON

TEAR OUT THIS PAGE AND TAPE IT TO CREATE A MEGAPHONE SO YOU CAN AMPLIFY YOUR VOICE WHEN YOU SCREAM YOUR FAVOURITE CURSE WORD

SARCASM

~~Kindness~~ is free – sprinkle it everywhere

RIGHTEOUS RAGE

You know the feeling you get when you *know* that you're right about something – with such *absolute certainty* you feel like you hold all the truths of the universe? Then you'll know that when you have that feeling there is nothing more infuriating than someone telling you you're wrong.

Think about the last time this happened to you, rant about it in the space below and wash the experience from your weary soul.

IT TAKES
43 MUSCLES
TO FROWN BUT
ZERO MUSCLES
FOR YOU TO
SHUT THE
HECK UP

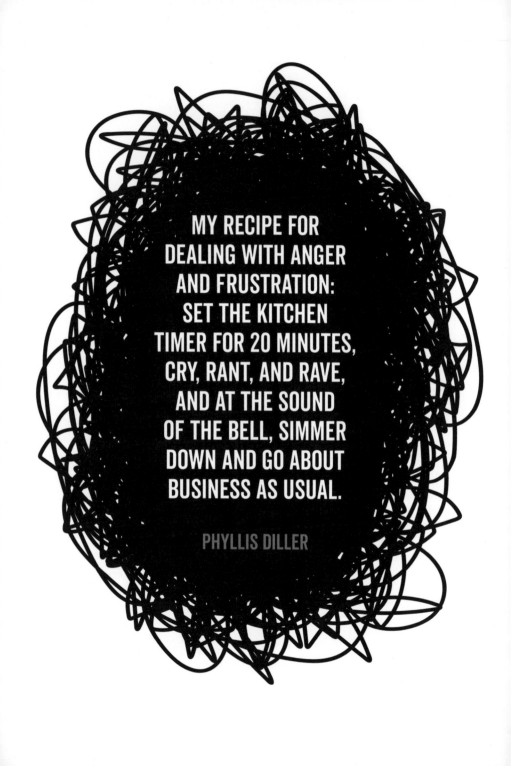

MY RECIPE FOR DEALING WITH ANGER AND FRUSTRATION: SET THE KITCHEN TIMER FOR 20 MINUTES, CRY, RANT, AND RAVE, AND AT THE SOUND OF THE BELL, SIMMER DOWN AND GO ABOUT BUSINESS AS USUAL.

PHYLLIS DILLER

TRASH TALK

Everyone has certain words that really rub them up the wrong way – words that, when we hear them, are the language equivalent of nails being scraped slowly down a giant blackboard. Think "claggy", "flaccid" or – the king of all the gross words – "moist". Use the space below to write down all the words and phrases that you hate and, therefore, need to get DIRECTLY into the bin.

IF YOU NEVER BELIEVE IN ANYTHING, YOU'LL NEVER BE DISAPPOINTED

STAB THIS PAGE WITH YOUR PEN AS MANY TIMES AS YOU CAN

Don't worry, I am just a page. I feel nothing.

It's a good day to have a ~~good day~~ **NAP**

THE AFTER-WRATH

You don't need a book to tell you that arguing makes you mad. Of course it does. Instead, this page is here to fix the "after-wrath" – the ill temper that you're left with after a particularly exasperating argument (you know – the kind where you're going around in circles and not being listened to, where you might as well be yelling at a loaf of bread for all the progress you're making). This page is for getting your side of the argument heard. Think back to your last shouting match, fill in the following sections and drive out the after-wrath once and for all.

What was the argument?

What is your perspective?

What did the other person claim?

The key to casting out the after-wrath is making a solid case against the opposition. This is the right moment to live the hot-shot lawyer fantasy, strutting around like nobody can tell you anything. Make your case. Defend your position. Say everything you didn't get a chance to say, laying down plainly why the opposition is deluded AF, and why you are right.

0/10 WOULD NOT RECOMMEND

This is another quick-fire round. Use the space below to write a list of all the food and drink items that you utterly despise: stuff that you never want to pass through your lips again; stuff that, if you were creating the world, you would cancel without a second thought. Goodbye.

1.

2.

3.

4.

5.

6.

7.

8.

9.

10.

"WOW –
ALL I NEEDED
TO TURN MY
LIFE AROUND
WAS YOUR
INSPIRATIONAL
QUOTE.
THANKS!" SAID
NOBODY EVER.

VOODOO DOLL TIME! WRITE A RAGE INSIDE THE DOLL, THEN DRAW PINS STABBING IT (MANY, MANY PINS.)

RAGE AGAINST PUBLIC TRANSPORT

Nobody knows which circle of hell public transport crawled out of, but that's beside the point. It's already here, causing problems and making lives terrible every day. Yes, it helps you to get from A to B, but *at what cost?* It's a veritable hotbed for awfulness and rage, and reliably brings out the worst, most infuriating behaviour in humankind. Do people sit too close to you for no reason? Do they take your reserved place and refuse to move? Has there ever been something suspicious and sticky on your seat, which you only realized was there after you'd been sitting on it for half an hour? Tell the book everything.

WORD SEARCH

Are you sick and tired of using the same old insults to express your outrage and disdain? Language loses its punch when it's used too often, so take inspiration from the days of yore and add to your vocabulary with some of the colourful offerings below. Then, find them in the word search opposite!

Loiter-sack (a lazy person)

Gnashgab (a person who complains)

Jobbernowl (a stupid person)

Fopdoodle (a foolish person)

Raggabrash (a disorganized person)

Cumberworld (a useless person)

Saddlegoose (a stupid person)

Knave (a dishonest person)

Mumblecrust (a toothless beggar)

Stampcrab (a clumsy person)

B	D	Y	I	L	O	Q	N	H	S	Q	E	V	M	H
B	T	J	L	A	W	R	H	B	A	L	L	U	T	S
O	B	D	V	X	M	O	T	S	D	H	M	L	P	A
A	D	W	Y	M	Q	B	N	O	D	B	O	G	N	R
C	U	M	B	E	R	W	O	R	L	D	Y	O	U	B
G	W	I	E	Q	H	D	O	E	E	J	S	G	G	A
N	B	W	S	K	P	Y	C	H	G	B	F	T	K	G
A	R	V	R	O	K	R	Y	X	O	C	B	N	K	G
S	B	C	F	B	U	F	U	U	O	Q	A	O	S	A
H	E	G	L	S	W	B	R	G	S	V	R	K	J	R
G	R	J	T	K	C	A	S	R	E	T	I	O	L	B
A	D	S	T	A	M	P	C	R	A	B	C	T	J	C
B	U	A	U	M	Z	V	J	B	Q	Q	V	H	F	K
F	B	N	A	E	B	A	J	A	H	F	D	Q	W	M
T	X	Y	U	K	H	B	E	N	N	P	X	K	X	Q

Be the reason
someone ~~smiles~~

LEAVES
YOU ALONE

NOT EVERYTHING HAPPENS FOR A

REASON.

SOMETIMES LIFE JUST

SUCKS.

ALEXA CHUNG

THE IDIOT AWARDS

Welcome to the Idiot Awards! Yes, this journal is awarding prizes in three categories: Idiot of the Week, Idiot of the Month and, finally, Idiot of the Year. The judging panel is made up of you, you and you. Use the space below to draw this prestigious award, then fill in the certificate for each lucky winner.

IDIOT OF THE WEEK

Name:

Reason for receiving the Idiot of the Week award:

Further comments:

IDIOT OF THE MONTH

Name:

Reason for receiving the Idiot of the Month award:

Further comments:

IDIOT OF THE YEAR

Name:

Reason for receiving the Idiot of the Year award:

Further comments:

TODAY GETS AN A FOR "AVERAGE"

TEAR OUT THIS PAGE AND MAKE IT INTO A PAPER PLANE. THEN THROW IT AT THE NEAREST WALL AS HARD AS YOU CAN. (AND IF YOU CAN'T MAKE A PAPER PLANE, JUST SCREW THE PAPER INTO A BALL BEFORE THROWING IT INSTEAD.)

I'm ready to fly!

I AM VERY POORLY
TODAY AND VERY
STUPID AND

HATE
EVERYBODY

AND EVERYTHING.

CHARLES DARWIN

JUSTICE IS SERVED

If someone else has made you feel bad and you're feeling the sting, then this is the page for you. The first thing to do is tell yourself that you have precisely NO TIME for people who make you feel bad. You deserve more than that. Okay?

The next thing to do is to grab your pen and prepare to write. Think about the event that's got you feeling this way and use the space below to detail exactly why the other person is wrong for acting the way they did. Write and write and write until you can let the moment go and feel better.

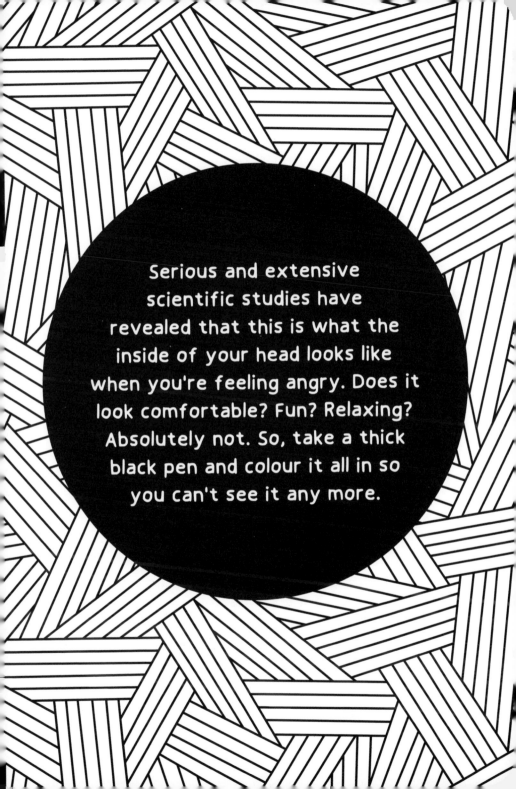

Serious and extensive scientific studies have revealed that this is what the inside of your head looks like when you're feeling angry. Does it look comfortable? Fun? Relaxing? Absolutely not. So, take a thick black pen and colour it all in so you can't see it any more.

THINGS WILL
PROBABLY
GET WORSE

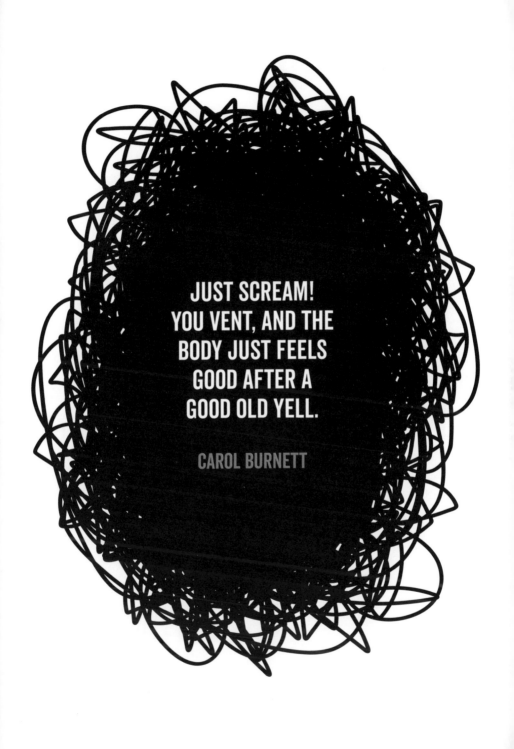

JUST SCREAM!
YOU VENT, AND THE
BODY JUST FEELS
GOOD AFTER A
GOOD OLD YELL.

CAROL BURNETT

LETTER OF COMPLAINT

Use the space below to write the most scathing letter of complaint that you can. Choose anyone or anything as your target: the chain restaurant that only gave you eight chicken nuggets when you should have had nine; your broadband provider whose Wi-Fi is too slow; the co-worker who shows you way too many pictures of their dog/holiday/kids. You shouldn't have to put up with any of this! Let the self-righteous outrage bubble up and then... off you go!

EVERY CLOUD HAS ANOTHER CLOUD WAITING JUST BEHIND IT

Always bring
your own
~~sunshine~~

SNACKS

YELL AT THIS PAGE AS LOUDLY AS YOU CAN

ROAD RAGE

The road is so famed for its anger-inducing qualities, it's already associated with "rage". However, everybody knows it's not good to vent your fury while you're behind the wheel, so take it out on this journal instead. Rate the following road crimes from one to five (one being "This is annoying" and five being "This makes me want to eat my own head").

RATING	1	2	3	4	5
Turning without indicating					
Hogging two parking spaces with one car					
Revving bikes so loudly you can't hear yourself think					
Keeping headlights at full beam					
Driving slowly in the fast lane					
Using the horn too much					
Tailgating					
Cyclists riding to the front of a traffic jam					
People who don't give you a courtesy wave when you've done them a favour					

Use the space below to chronicle your own tales of road rage, woe and fury:

_____

_____

_____

_____

_____

_____

_____

_____

_____

_____

_____

_____

_____

_____

_____

_____

_____

_____

Happy
people make
other people
~~happy~~

ANGRY

STUPIDITY... IS THE
BASIC BUILDING BLOCK
OF THE UNIVERSE.

FRANK ZAPPA

FASHION NONSENSE

Fashion is a way to express your taste and your sense of style. Unfortunately, some people have none. Every day, a bunch of really terrible choices are made in the wardrobe department, which just make you want to throw your hands up and shout, "WHY ARE YOU DOING THIS TO YOURSELF?" Instead of shouting at innocent people, draw your outrage below. What are the fashion choices that make you shudder? What sartorial crimes have you witnessed recently?

POM-POM
STRESS BUSTER

It's time to get crafty. This pom-pom stress buster could be your saving grace in times of need.

You will need: cardboard, scissors, yarn, needle and thread, and nimble fingers.

Cut out two cardboard discs of equal size – the bigger the disc, the bigger the pom-pom. Cut a small hole in the middle of each disc, big enough to pass the yarn through, and lay them on top of each other. Loop the yarn through the holes and around the outer edges of the discs, holding it in place with your fingers to begin with to make sure it doesn't unravel. Repeat until the discs are completely covered. Place the scissors between the two discs of cardboard and cut through the yarn on the outer edge. Carefully wrap a piece of thread between the discs and tie a knot to hold the pom-pom together. Once the yarn is securely tied, cut the cardboard and pull it away from the pom-pom.

Nailed it.

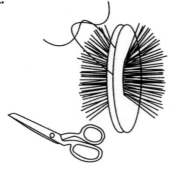

GO WITH THE FLOW. OR DON'T. IT DOESN'T REALLY MATTER.

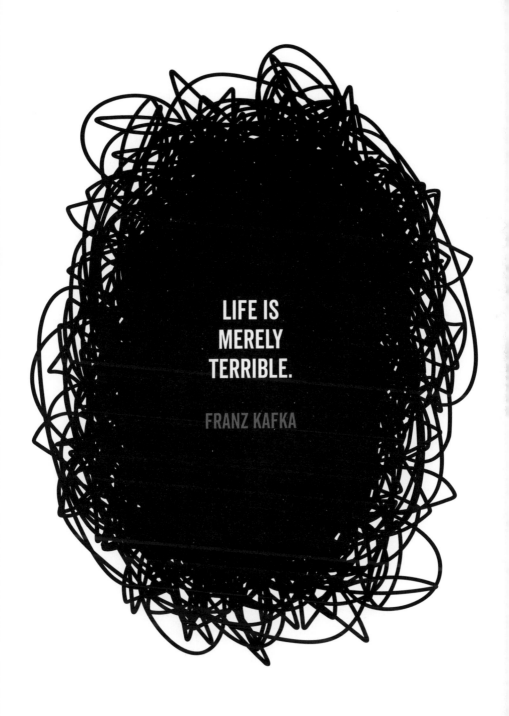

LIFE IS
MERELY
TERRIBLE.

FRANZ KAFKA

GONE BUT NOT FORGOTTEN

Picture the scene: your favourite product gets discontinued. A beloved TV show gets the axe. In these situations it's hard to know whether to be angry or sad, so you end up being a weird and unsatisfying combination of both. What you really need to do is rage-mourn. Fill in the page below to cast off the weird feeling. Be angry at your loss and grieve for what could have been.

RAGE-MOURN 1

RIP to:

Left me when:

You will be remembered as:

RAGE-MOURN 2

RIP to:

Left me when:

You will be remembered as:

RAGE-MOURN 3

RIP to:

Left me when:

You will be remembered as:

RAGE-MOURN 4

RIP to:

Left me when:

You will be remembered as:

EVERYTHING
HAPPENS FOR
NO REASON

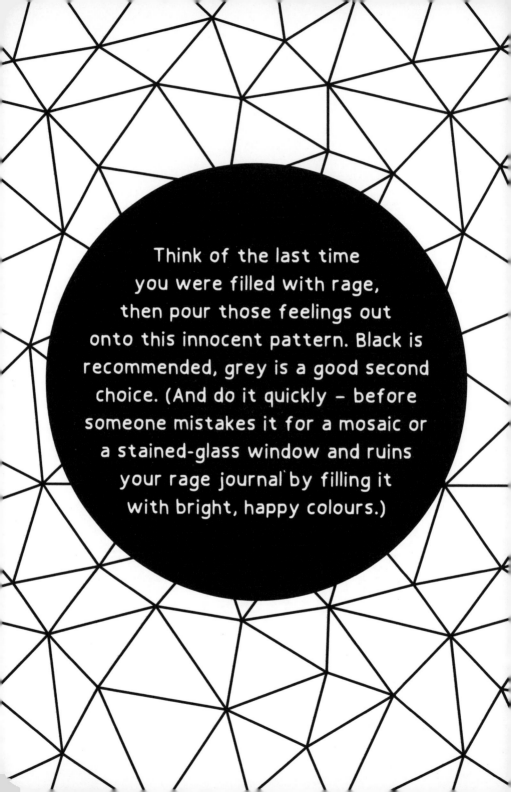

Think of the last time
you were filled with rage,
then pour those feelings out
onto this innocent pattern. Black is
recommended, grey is a good second
choice. (And do it quickly – before
someone mistakes it for a mosaic or
a stained-glass window and ruins
your rage journal by filling it
with bright, happy colours.)

SORROW AND SHAME UPON YOUR HEAD!

RUIN UPON ALL

BELONGING TO YOU!

CHARLES DICKENS

POINTLESS RAGE

What are the absolute stupidest things that you rage about? We're not talking about the small stuff that can be justified, like stubbing your toe, or the "tear here" tab breaking off your pack of cookies before you've been able to open them. We're talking about the *really* stupid stuff. The things that are so stupid that feeling any anger at all is completely irrational. Maybe you hate the number 26. Or mustard-yellow cushions. Or the sight of clean washing you now have to fold. The thing is, even though you know you shouldn't be mad about these things, it doesn't change the fact that *they do make you mad*. Let loose on the page below and list all those irrational, petty, ultra-dumb things that somehow make you want to flip a table.

TAKE THE BOOK OUTSIDE AND RUB THIS PAGE ALONG THE GROUND

Good things come to ~~those who wait~~

THE MOST ANNOYING PEOPLE

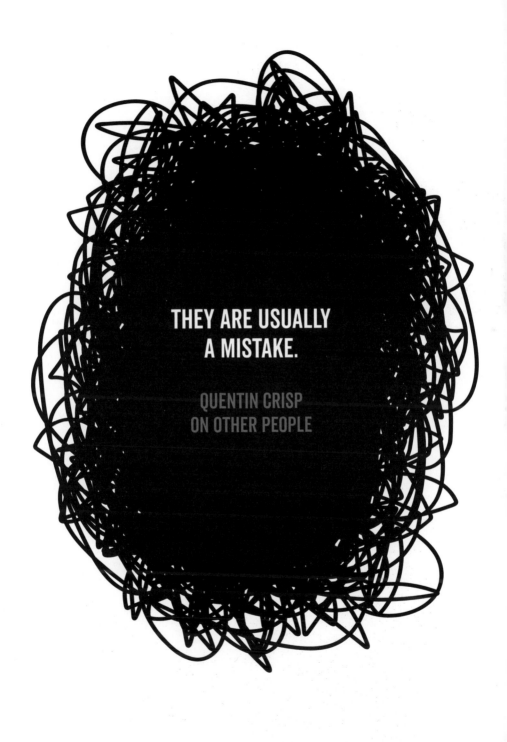

THEY ARE USUALLY
A MISTAKE.

QUENTIN CRISP
ON OTHER PEOPLE

SOCIAL-MEDIA SINNERS

Everybody knows that social media is a bin fire of nonsense. When people get behind a keyboard and a screen, something happens that makes them forget how to behave like fully functioning human beings. Common sense is thrown so far out of the window it's launched into deep space.

All you want to do is read a message or enjoy some sweet, mindless scrolling time, but it's impossible to do so without being bombarded with inane notifications and wading through updates you don't give a toss about. Urgh.

Take the edge off the rage with this game of social-media bingo. Cross off each square when you see it.

Vacuous, clichéd captions ("Drinks with this one" or "Take me back")	People asking you to like their friend's brother's music page on Facebook	When people leave you on read	"Copy and paste this as your status if... "
People who share every post they read	People asking questions they could just google	Couples with a joint profile	Cryptic, attention-seeking statuses
Hundreds of holiday photos	People who tag themselves at the airport	People who very publicly announce they're going on a "social media detox"	Mediocre pictures of food
People who post inspirational quotes	Obviously staged candid photos	People using social media like a diary	People who post the results of novelty personality quizzes

THE BURN UNIT

There's a time and a place for sarcastic comments and snarky comebacks: it's here and it's now! Think back to all the rage-inducing moments where you've had to hold your tongue, and think about all the things that you so dearly wished you had said. Then, fill in the incident cards below to dish out burns so hot they'll need to be run under cold water for at least 20 minutes.

INCIDENT 1

Who was involved:

Incident:

Burning comeback:

INCIDENT 2

Who was involved:

Incident:

Burning comeback:

INCIDENT 3

Who was involved:

Incident:

Burning comeback:

INCIDENT 4

Who was involved:

Incident:

Burning comeback:

WORD SEARCH

When you're angry, sometimes the best thing to do is distract yourself. Quick: find the word **"potato"** in the word search below!

T	A	O	A	T	P	T	A	A	P	O	T	O	A	T
A	T	P	O	T	A	T	A	P	P	A	O	T	T	O
P	O	A	A	A	T	O	O	A	T	T	A	O	P	A
A	P	T	T	A	P	O	T	T	O	A	P	P	A	A
O	A	A	O	P	O	T	A	O	T	A	P	A	O	O
A	T	O	P	A	A	T	O	O	A	P	O	P	P	A
T	T	A	P	O	T	A	A	P	T	T	O	A	T	A
P	O	P	A	A	O	T	T	A	A	T	T	P	P	O
T	T	A	O	P	P	O	A	P	A	P	O	T	A	T
O	O	P	T	A	T	O	P	T	T	O	P	P	A	T
T	A	A	O	P	T	A	O	A	P	P	A	O	O	P
T	P	O	P	A	T	T	A	O	A	T	P	P	T	A
A	P	T	A	T	O	O	T	P	A	O	P	T	A	T
P	O	A	T	O	A	P	P	A	O	T	O	P	T	A
O	T	T	O	P	P	T	O	P	T	A	A	T	O	P

YOU MUST HAVE MISTAKEN ME FOR SOMEONE WHO GIVES A TOSS

STAMP ON
THIS PAGE

TOILET-PAPER WARS

There are few subjects more highly debated than the correct way to position your toilet paper. The million–dollar question: do you position the roll so the paper hangs down the front or the back of the roll? The only thing that's clear in an argument of this scale and intensity is there are two camps: people who are right and the deluded, senseless FOOLS who are not. Draw the correct configuration of TP below to establish your dominance and indisputable RIGHT–ness.

Now that you've cleared up the issue once and for all, it's time to take the culprits to task. Fill in the lines below with all the miscreants who you know for a fact hang the toilet paper the wrong way round. Or, as they are also known, criminals.

LIVE IN THE NO

WHY DOES THE UNIVERSE GO TO ALL THE BOTHER OF

EXISTING?

STEPHEN HAWKING

INNOCENT (AND RAGING)

Does anything get you more riled up than being blamed for something you didn't do? Whether it's something as small and inconsequential as a fart, or as serious and life-threatening as forgetting to switch off the living-room light when you left the house, being blamed for something you know you didn't do is the TOTAL worst and can fill you with day-ruining rage. Vent your furious feelings of injustice on the page below.

CRIMES I AM INNOCENT OF:

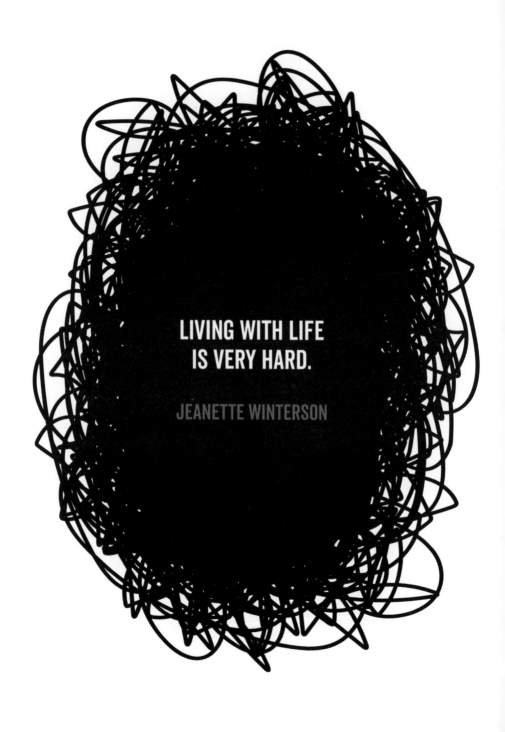

First,
dream it,
then,
~~do it~~

FORGET IT

MOST-WANTED LIST

The first rule of life is: never eat yellow snow. The second rule is: never lend your stuff to other people, because you will never see that stuff again. Most people learn this the hard way, and you probably did as well, which is precisely why this page is here in the rage journal.

Think of all the items that have been thoughtlessly spirited away from right under your nose, by the people you trusted most. Think back on all the happy memories you had with those possessions. Remember owning them? Remember the heady joy of knowing you could read that book, wear that top, use that piece of gardening equipment whenever you wanted?

Well, now it's payback time. Fill out the wanted posters below and demand some JUSTICE.

Name:

Also known as:

Distinguishing features:

Last seen:

Wanted for:

Reward:

Name:

Also known as:

Distinguishing features:

Last seen:

Wanted for:

Reward:

Name:

Also known as:

Distinguishing features:

Last seen:

Wanted for:

Reward:

Name:

Also known as:

Distinguishing features:

Last seen:

Wanted for:

Reward:

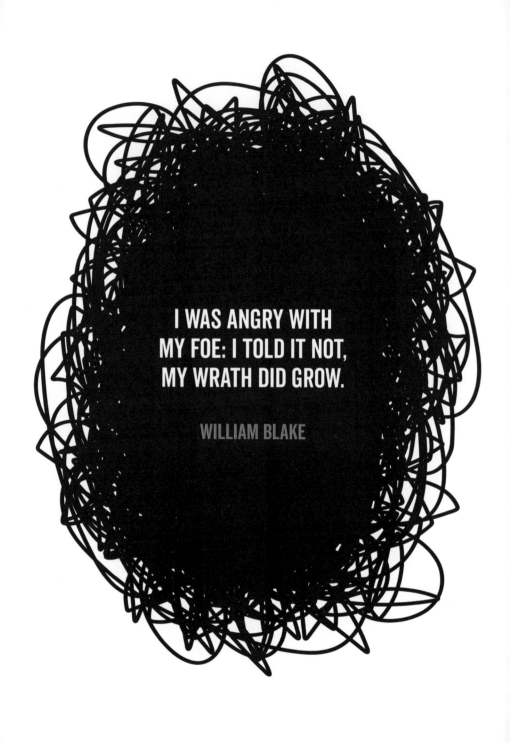

I WAS ANGRY WITH
MY FOE: I TOLD IT NOT,
MY WRATH DID GROW.

WILLIAM BLAKE

RIP THIS
PAGE INTO
PIECES...
BUT DO IT
S-L-O-W-L-Y

Tear meeee.

WISH I WASN'T HERE

List all the places that you utterly despise. You could be general, declaring your contempt for entire cities, or you could get really specific ("The middle toilet cubicle at work" or "My mother-in-law's tacky living room"). Don't think too deeply about this round. Gut instinct will lead the way.

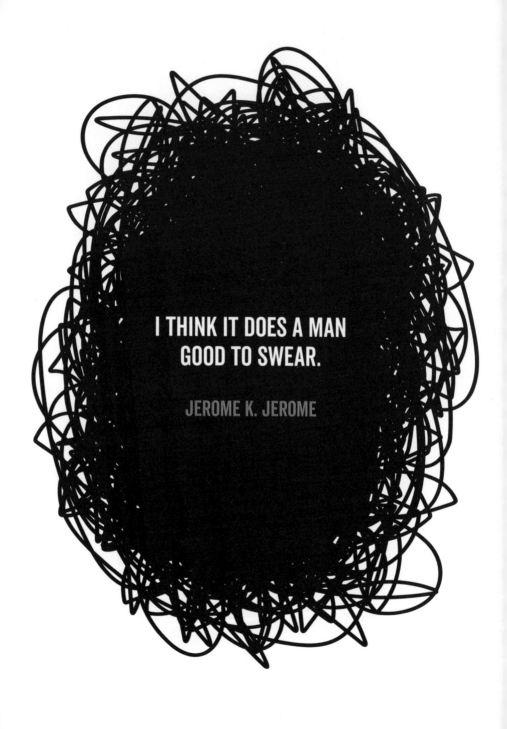

I THINK IT DOES A MAN
GOOD TO SWEAR.

JEROME K. JEROME

WHAT DOESN'T KILL ME USUALLY JUST MAKES ME ANGRY

NINETY PER CENT OF EVERYTHING IS

CRAP.

THEODORE STURGEON

PUNCH A HOLE IN THIS PAGE

Yep. Nothing on this side. Just punch right through.

WHY ARE YOU THE WAY YOU ARE?

Is there anything worse than other people? No. The answer is no. Other people are out there, every day, and they are deliberately trying to make your life a living hell by doing things like having bare feet in public, unleashing audibly wet sneezes in your vicinity or being sickeningly positive and chirpy. But this time, other people are not going to succeed in ruining your day, because you are going to pin their misdeeds to this page instead.

THE WORST THINGS ABOUT OTHER PEOPLE:

**PLEASE
GO AWAY**

TEAR OUT THIS PAGE AND BURN IT*

*In a burn-proof metal or glass bowl, or in a fireplace. Safety first, rage second.

Burn, baby, burn.

I BELIEVE
I CAN, BUT
I DON'T WANT
TO, SO I WON'T

When
opportunity
knocks,
~~open the door~~

WAIT FOR
IT TO
LEAVE

I DON'T HATE PEOPLE. I JUST FEEL BETTER WHEN THEY

AREN'T AROUND.

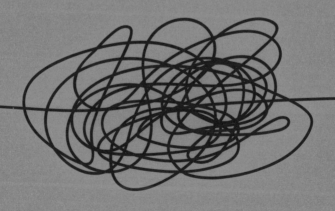

CHARLES BUKOWSKI

THINGS I WILL NEVER DO AGAIN

Karaoke with colleagues. Eating olives. Putting milk into the bowl BEFORE the cereal. List all the things that you will NEVER do again on the basis of them being terrible.

NEVER GO TO BED MAD –
STAY UP AND FIGHT.

PHYLLIS DILLER

You are

capable of

~~incredible~~

~~things~~

SOME

THINGS

CRUSH THIS PAGE. JUST TAKE IT IN YOUR FIST AND CRUSH IT.

Go for it!

I WOULD LIKE TO CONFIRM THAT I DO NOT CARE

SAY "NO" TO BEING ZEN

Unfortunately, as you go through life, it's inevitable that you'll meet people who don't embrace the cathartic philosophy of this book. When you're boiling with everyday rage and ready to blow, they'll tell you to lighten up, to just smile and to take a few deep breaths, push the anger down and just carry on...

Use this page to prepare some responses to those infuriating people who think being zen is the answer to everything. Next time you encounter one, you'll be ready.

TURN YOUR FACE TO THE SUN AND YOU'LL JUST HAVE THE SUN IN YOUR EYES

DELETE TEN

This is the final prompt in the book, and it's all about cleaning up, starting fresh and making the world a better, less angry place. Fill out the page below, answering the following question: if you could delete ten things from your life, what would they be?

1. _____

2. _____

3. _____

4. _____

5. _____

6. _____

7. _____

8. _____

9. _____

10. _____

YOU INSPIRE ME...
TO BE NOTHING
LIKE YOU

Never let

~~your fear~~

MOTIVATIONAL
QUOTES

decide your

future

CONCLUSION

Congratulations – you've reached the end of the journal! Do you feel better?

The book might be looking a little worse for wear, but hopefully your mood should be improved. After releasing all your everyday anger into the pages of this journal, you should now be able to breathe a sigh of relief and let it all go.

(Until the next person cuts in front of you in a queue, that is...)

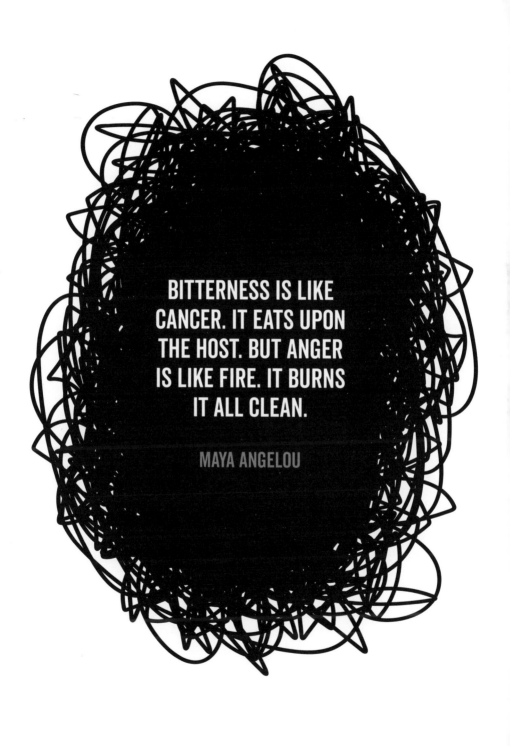

BITTERNESS IS LIKE
CANCER. IT EATS UPON
THE HOST. BUT ANGER
IS LIKE FIRE. IT BURNS
IT ALL CLEAN.

MAYA ANGELOU

If you're interested in finding out more about our books,
find us on Facebook at Summersdale Publishers
and follow us on Twitter at @Summersdale.

www.summersdale.com

WORD SEARCH ANSWERS

Page 19:

S	T	T	I	U	A	H	E	J	H	D	W	B	C	K
P	O	N	I	V	N	K	E	O	B	Q	H	Z	N	C
M	D	N	E	E	C	M	L	C	F	A	A	U	E	A
H	T	C	O	Z	G	Y	V	L	K	D	T	S	F	R
R	K	Z	O	F	S	D	P	Z	R	O	T	E	Y	F
W	M	X	P	H	A	S	U	A	X	A	H	G	Q	N
G	M	J	E	E	Y	B	G	F	V	R	E	Q	O	E
A	Q	E	R	R	J	U	U	J	R	O	D	J	U	G
H	T	U	T	W	S	F	D	C	W	L	U	Z	L	X
L	S	H	O	O	T	W	Q	K	K	D	C	N	Q	L
B	W	H	S	Y	N	A	Y	L	U	E	K	B	I	R
Z	Z	N	Q	S	B	O	Y	U	J	I	T	U	Z	W
M	O	T	H	E	R	T	R	U	C	K	E	R	B	K
T	I	K	C	U	L	P	H	T	B	J	L	F	C	N
Q	C	J	W	G	J	I	Y	K	F	L	F	B	T	E

Page 83:

B	D	Y	I	L	O	Q	N	H	S	Q	E	V	M	H
B	T	J	L	A	W	R	H	B	A	L	L	U	T	S
O	B	D	V	X	M	O	T	S	D	H	M	L	P	A
A	D	W	Y	M	Q	B	N	O	D	B	O	G	N	R
C	U	M	B	E	R	W	O	R	L	D	Y	O	U	B
G	W	I	E	Q	H	D	O	E	E	J	S	G	G	A
N	B	W	S	K	P	Y	C	H	G	B	F	T	K	G
A	R	V	R	O	K	R	Y	X	O	C	B	N	K	G
S	B	C	F	B	U	F	U	U	O	Q	A	O	S	A
H	E	G	L	S	W	B	R	G	S	V	R	K	J	R
G	R	J	T	K	C	A	S	R	E	T	I	O	L	B
A	D	S	T	A	M	P	C	R	A	B	C	T	J	C
B	U	A	U	M	Z	V	J	B	Q	Q	V	H	F	K
F	B	N	A	E	B	A	J	A	H	F	D	Q	W	M
T	X	Y	U	K	H	B	E	N	N	P	X	K	X	Q

Page 119:

T	A	O	A	T	P	T	A	A	P	O	T	O	A	T
A	T	P	O	T	A	T	A	P	P	A	O	T	T	O
P	O	A	A	A	T	O	O	A	T	T	A	O	P	A
A	P	T	T	A	P	O	T	T	O	A	P	P	A	A
O	A	A	O	P	O	T	A	O	T	A	P	A	O	O
A	T	O	P	A	A	T	O	O	A	P	O	P	P	A
T	T	A	P	O	T	A	A	P	T	T	O	A	T	A
P	O	P	A	A	O	T	T	A	A	T	T	P	P	O
T	T	A	O	P	P	O	A	P	A	P	O	T	A	T
O	O	P	T	A	T	O	P	T	T	O	P	P	A	T
T	A	A	O	P	T	A	O	A	P	P	A	O	O	P
T	P	O	P	A	T	T	A	O	A	T	P	P	T	A
A	P	T	A	T	O	O	T	P	A	O	P	T	A	T
P	O	A	T	O	A	P	P	A	O	T	O	P	T	A
O	T	T	O	P	P	P	T	O	P	T	A	A	T	O	P

IMAGE CREDITS

Arrow pattern background © Sunspire/
Shutterstock.com; Bin © rangsan
paidaen/Shutterstock.com; Megaphone
© Giamportone/Shutterstock.com;
Mosaic pattern background © TANANR23/
Shutterstock.com; Notepaper © Antonov
Maxim/Shutterstock.com; Picture frames ©
Maaike Boot/Shutterstock.com; Social media
icons © AllNikArt/Shutterstock.com; Spade
© Yevgen Kravchenko/Shutterstock.com;
Straight line pattern background © anfisa
focusova/Shutterstock.com; Voodoo doll
© Vector Icons/Shutterstock.com